THE BATTLE OF

GETTYSBURG

Author
Colin Hynson
Consultant
Dr Richard Tames

ticktock

THE CAST

Abraham Lincoln *1809-65. Lincoln was voted in as a Republican President in 1860. He wanted freedom for American slaves which made him unpopular in the South, where there were almost 4 million slaves. This was one of the causes for the civil war. After the North's victory Lincoln wrote the Emancipation Proclomation which freed the slaves.*

Jefferson Davis *1808-89. Davis was elected President of the Confederate States of America. These states had removed themselves from the United States of America because they did not agree with the politics of Abraham Lincoln. He commanded the Confederate army but is thought to have made bad decisions which led to their defeat.*

Robert E. Lee *1807-1870. A US general, Lee was made Commander -in-Chief of the Confederate Army of Virginia. He led his army to victory against the Unionists many times. However, his defeat at Gettysburg was the beginning of the end for the Confederate army. Two months later Lee surrendered his army to General Grant.*

Ulysses Grant *1822-85. A US general, Grant was promoted to major general during the war. He was a talented military man who led the Union army to several important victories. He was also fair-minded and refused to humiliate the Confederates after their defeat.*

George G. Meade *1815-72. He took over from General Hooker as commander of the Union Army of the Potomac. He proved to be a strong leader and won several vital battles. The most important of these was his defence against Pickett's Charge by the Confederates.*

Thomas J. Jackson *1824-63. Also known as Stonewall Jackson, this Confederate general was one of Robert E. Lee's favourites. His brilliant tactics won the Confederate army several successes. Jackson was accidently killed by his own men after they mistook him for a Union soldier.*

Copyright © ticktock Entertainment Ltd 2006
First published in Great Britain in 2006 by ticktock Media Ltd.,
Unit 2, Orchard Business Centre, North Farm Road, Tunbridge Wells, Kent, TN2 3XF
ISBN 1 84696 002 9
Printed in China
A CIP catalogue record for this book is available from the British Library.

CONTENTS

AN INDEPENDENT AMERICA 4
• *New Government* • *George Washington becomes the first President*
• *The Louisiana Purchase*

SLAVERY 6
• *Ban on slaves imports* • *Southern Agriculture and Northern Industrialisation*
• *North and South Divide*

NORTH VS SOUTH 12
• *Two Presidents One Country* • *Civil War Divides America*
• *Confederacy Victories*

ARRIVAL AT GETTYSBURG 20
• *The Battle at McPherson's Ridge* • *More Confederate Wins and Union Losses*
• *Battle of Oak Hill*

GETTYSBURG DAY TWO 26
• *The Battle at Devil's Den* • *The Confederates Take Big Round Top*
• *Union Victory at Little Round Top*

GETTYSBURG DAY THREE 32
• *Artillery Attack, Pickett's Charge* • *Unionists Win the War*
• *The Gettysburg Address*

TIMELINE & DID YOU KNOW? 44

GLOSSARY 46

INDEX 48

AN INDEPENDENT AMERICA

In 1783 American rebels won their independence from Britain. However, they now had to decide what kind of government they wanted for their new country. It took five years for the Constitution of the United States to be agreed.

Mr George Washington, we, the Congress of the United States, ask you to become the first President of the United States.

I accept your invitation. Now we must look forwards and secure the future of our new country.

For the next few decades America grew in the west and the south. In 1803 the United States bought a huge area of land from the French. This was known as the Louisiana Purchase.

Have you heard how much land we bought? I'm told it is nearly one million square miles.

Yes! And we only paid fifteen million dollars.

LOUISANA PURCHASE

The Louisiana Purchase meant that there were new territories to explore. In 1804 Meriwether Lewis and William Clark were sent to map the new territory, west of the Mississippi River.

This map shows how the United States of America looked in 1860. It grew quickly from the original thirteen states on the east coast taken from Britain in 1783.

SLAVERY

In 1808 it became illegal in America to bring slaves in from abroad. However, the number of slaves still grew. They were not regarded as human beings, but as the property of slave-owners.

Most of the slaves in America worked on vast cotton fields in the south of the country.

The sun has not gone down yet. We have many more hours to go.

How much longer do we have to work?

Because slaves were seen as property they were often treated cruelly.

This will teach you to be lazy.

***Stop!** Where are you going?*

The slave-owners of the south believed that slavery was good for everybody, including the slaves.

Thousands of slaves ran away to the North of America where they would be free.

Of course we need our slaves. They work in our fields and homes. We treat them well. We provide them with food and somewhere to live.

By the 1820s there were clear differences between the north and south of the United States. In the south agriculture, particularly cotton, drove the economy. The Mississippi River was an important area for cotton growing.

At the same time, large factories began to appear in the north of the United States. Alongside them towns and cities grew.

Manufacturing. That's the future of this country.

And free labour. We don't need slaves in our factories.

FAST FACT The first steam-powered cotton mill starts work in Massachusetts in 1847.

The railway arrived in America in 1830. It spread westwards from all points along the east coast.

Look at that! These locomotives will bring our country much closer together.

Yes, and it means we won't need the rivers to carry our goods anymore.

Gradually north and south started to divide. It was not just differences of opinion about slavery or the different economies that separated them. There was also the problem of who held the most power, would it be individual states or central government?

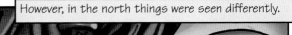

However, in the north things were seen differently.

We cannot allow these southerners to ignore the government, just because they do not like what is decided.

What is worse, they are threatening to leave the Union if they do not get their way.

That is blackmail. *The will of the whole country should prevail.*

FAST FACT The three main crops in the south were cotton, indigo and tobacco.

When Abraham Lincoln became President in 1860, most of the southern states left the United States. They formed the Confederate States of America and made Jefferson Davis President. The split between the north and south United States seemed impossible to fix.

And I tell you that, as your new President, I will not allow Lincoln or his northern friends to force us to be part of a country that has turned against us.

On April 12, 1861 the first shots of the American Civil War were fired. They came from confederate soldiers trying to stop supplies getting through to government-controlled Fort Sumter.

Fire up there! We have to prevent the supplies from getting through.

Soon after the first major battle between the two sides took place, on July 21, 1861 in Virginia. It was called the First Battle of the Bull Run. The battle was fierce with close hand-to-hand fighting.

We have to drive the Union soldiers back. If we win today then we will win the war.

Ordinary people, supporting the Union soldiers were watching the battle. Some of them even brought picnics with them.

However, the Union troops were driven back by Confederate reinforcements. They retreated straight through the shocked civilians.

Are those our troops? Have we lost the day?

How could this have happened?

The next important battle took place in New Orleans. As the largest city in the south of the United States it was very important. Whichever side controlled New Orleans also controlled the mighty Mississippi River that the Confederates used to ship their supplies.

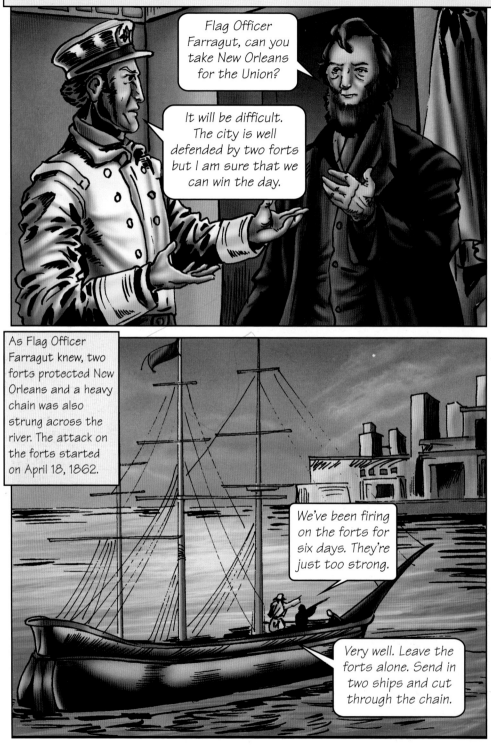

Flag Officer Farragut, can you take New Orleans for the Union?

It will be difficult. The city is well defended by two forts but I am sure that we can win the day.

As Flag Officer Farragut knew, two forts protected New Orleans and a heavy chain was also strung across the river. The attack on the forts started on April 18, 1862.

We've been firing on the forts for six days. They're just too strong.

Very well. Leave the forts alone. Send in two ships and cut through the chain.

Farragut's ships cut through the chain and sailed on to New Orleans. On 25th April he demanded the surrender of the now defenceless city.

Lay down your arms. We have come to accept your surrender of New Orleans.

You can take our buildings but we will never surrender.

The American Civil War was the first war in which iron ships replaced wooden ones. Both sides used them throughout the entire war. The first iron-clad ship used by the Confederates was called Virginia, and the Union's ship was named Monitor. They both saw action at the Battle of Hampton Roads in the spring of 1862.

During 1862 the Confederate armies were doing well but the Union army was making little progress. The Union General Joseph Hooker promised to reverse Union fortunes.

The Confederates have slowed our advance. We need another victory.

Then I shall give you one! I am planning to challenge General Lee and his army very soon.

In April 1862 General Hooker amassed a huge army of 130,000 men and marched to meet General Lee's army in Virginia.

Follow me, men. There are only 60,000 Confederate soldiers against us. This will be an easy victory.

60,000? We have double that number. I'm looking forward to this.

The two armies met at Chancellorsville, Virginia on May 2nd. General Hooker did not know that General Lee had been joined by another Confederate army led by General Stonewall Jackson.

Charge!

Look! We weren't told we have to fight two armies.

We've surprised them. The Union soldiers weren't expecting us to be here.

The battle lasted three days and Hooker's men suffered heavy casualties. They were forced to retreat.

However, the Confederate army also lost many men and one of General Lee's best leaders was accidentally killed by his own side.

Don't shoot! Don't shoot! You're firing at General Jackson.

Up there! Union soldiers.

Aaargh

FAST FACT

There were 30,000 casualties during the Batttle of Chancellorville.

General Lee wanted to take advantage of his victory at Chancellorsville.

We have to move north. The Union armies are in disarray. We can take advantage of this.

Then we must move fast. We cannot give the Union time to organise themselves.

There were other reasons why the Confederates were looking for a quick victory.

I know, but General Lee is pushing forwards. Once the British and French see we are winning then they will come to our side.

President Davis. We need the support of Europe if we are going to win this war.

The Union troops also needed victory to boost their morale.

I'm hungry. We've been promised more supplies and they haven't arrived yet.

We should have defeated the Confederates by now. I want to get home to my family.

President Lincoln was unhappy with General Hooker and in June 1863 decided to replace him.

General Meade, I want you to take charge of our military strategy. We need to start winning again.

You can rely on me, Mr President. We shall soon be victorious.

FAST FACT Soldiers on both sides were so hungry that they would steal food from local farms.

ARRIVAL AT GETTYSBURG

At the end of June General Lee moved his troops northwards towards the small town of Gettysburg in Pennsylvania to meet General Meade's Union army. The first time they came face-to-face was on June 30th when Confederate troops entered the town searching for supplies.

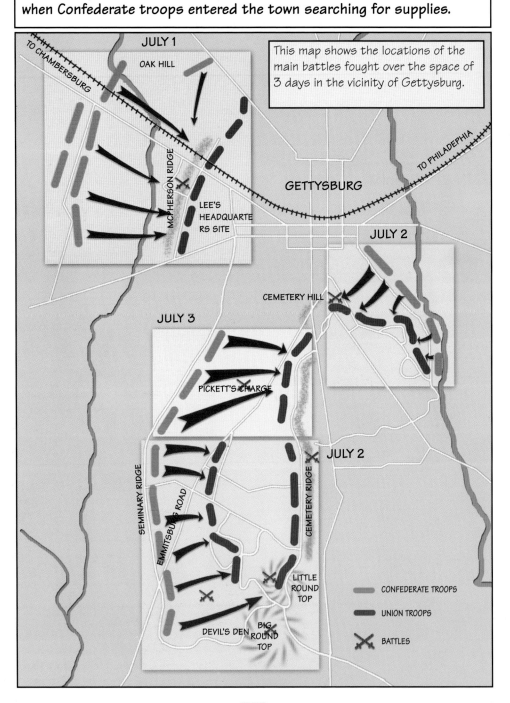

This map shows the locations of the main battles fought over the space of 3 days in the vicinity of Gettysburg.

JULY 1

TO CHAMBERSBURG

OAK HILL

MCPHERSON RIDGE

LEE'S HEADQUARTERS SITE

GETTYSBURG

TO PHILADEPHIA

CEMETERY HILL

JULY 2

JULY 3

PICKETT'S CHARGE

JULY 2

SEMINARY RIDGE

EMMITSBURG ROAD

CEMETERY RIDGE

LITTLE ROUND TOP

DEVIL'S DEN

BIG ROUND TOP

CONFEDERATE TROOPS

UNION TROOPS

BATTLES

The next day, July 1st, was the first real battle between the two sides. The Union General John Reynolds was in the thick of the fighting.

Come on you men. We have to drive the Confederates out of this town.

Charge!

However, the Confederate troops fought well. One musket shot gave them a huge advantage.

It's the Union General Reynolds. **Fire!**

Aaargh

General Reynolds was killed instantly.

FAST FACT After General Reynolds was killed almost 60% of his men were killed or wounded in the battle that followed.

Fighting on the first day focused around two areas, a deep cut around the railroad and McPherson's Ridge. Control of the railroad cut was important to both sides.

23

The Union leader Major-General Winfield Hancock tried to rally his troops.

Sir, we have just had a message. The Confederates are pushing our troops back from McPherson's Ridge.

Tell our troops to hold their ground for a while longer. I shall organise their retreat.

Confederate troops began to gain ground around McPherson's Ridge and also Cemetery Hill.

Confederates. They're coming towards us.

Fire into the woods. We have the Union soldiers trapped in there.

Major-General Hancock brought order back to what might have been a chaotic retreat by Union soldiers.

On the second day of fighting, the Confederates made more gains. Until, Union troops spotted Confederate troops marching along Emmitsburg Road.

Again there was close hand-to-hand fighting on a rocky hill known as the Devil's Den.

The Union troops knew that they had to keep the high ground around Gettysburg if they wanted to stop the Confederate advance.

The cannons had the effect the Confederates wanted. Now they were ready to charge up Big Round Top.

The Confederates took Big Round Top from the Union side. They celebrated their success.

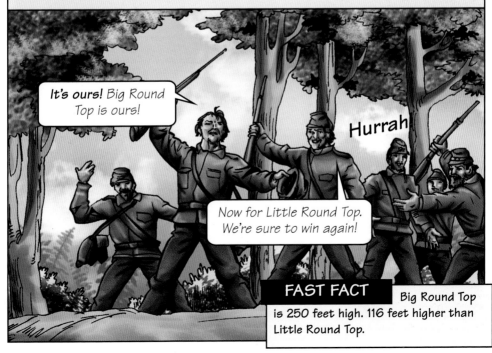

FAST FACT Big Round Top is 250 feet high. 116 feet higher than Little Round Top.

The Union General Gouverneur Warren could see what the Confederates were planning.

They've taken Big Round Top. We must reinforce Little Round Top now.

Those Union soldiers won't know what's hit them.

Charge!

Just one more attack, lads. Up that hill.

Driven on by their success at Big Round Top, the Confederates charged Little Round Top.

This time the Union troops were better prepared. They ran down the hill towards the Confederate soldiers.

Fix bayonets and charge men!

We've lost the attack. **Run.**

Push the Confederates back. **Push them back.**

The Confederate troops were pushed back from their positions by Union soldiers.

Come on men. We have to regroup. The Union army might have won this fight but we will win the battle.

How could we have lost that hill? We were so close to victory.

On the third day of the Battle of Gettysburg the Confederate leader General Lee decided to take the initiative after his losses the day before.

General Pickett lined up his Confederate troops and began marching them towards Union lines at Cemetery Ridge. He ordered them to maintain a steady walking pace.

Casualties were heavy among the Confederate soldiers as artillery and gun fire rained down on them.

The Confederate troops started slowing down and bunching together. General Kemper rode forward to urge them on.

Come on men! Keep marching forward. Don't slow down. You **can** reach those Union lines.

Just then General Kemper was shot.

When they saw General Kemper fall the Confederate soldiers lost all discipline and just ran at the Union lines.

They've killed General Kemper.

Let's get them. Let's get to those Union lines.

The Confederate troops reached the Union lines. Most of the Union soldiers were artillery troops and did not have any rifles to fight with.

Finally, Union soldiers arrived to support the artillery troops. They fixed bayonets and charged. The Confederate troops retreated leaving nearly 1000 soldiers dead or wounded.

FAST FACT The last attack on the retreating Confederates was on July 14th.

The Confederate troops marched away from Gettysburg as a defeated army. Union troops continued to pursue them.

The Battle of Gettysburg paved the way for the final defeat of the Confederate cause. On July 4th General Lee admitted defeat to his officers.

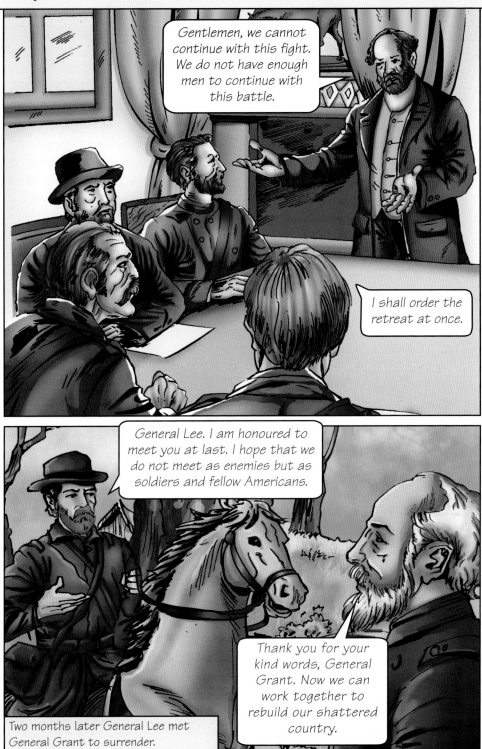

Gentlemen, we cannot continue with this fight. We do not have enough men to continue with this battle.

I shall order the retreat at once.

General Lee. I am honoured to meet you at last. I hope that we do not meet as enemies but as soldiers and fellow Americans.

Thank you for your kind words, General Grant. Now we can work together to rebuild our shattered country.

Two months later General Lee met General Grant to surrender.

The American Civil War finally ended in April 1865 when Generals Grant and Lee met at the Appomattox Court House in Virginia on April 9th. As General Lee left the Court House after surrendering to General Grant, the Union troops guarding the building began to jeer.

General Grant came out to talk to them. He told the soldiers that Union forces should not gloat over a defeated enemy, and that their enemies of yesterday were now their brothers.

America paid a heavy price for four years of war. Over half a million people died and the ecomony of the south of the country was devastated.

The Union soldiers passed through here just a few months ago. They destroyed my crops and my house. What am I going to do?

One group of people who benefited from the end of the Civil War were the four million slaves. Victory for the Union meant freedom for them. Many of them left the cotton plantations to work in the cities in the north of the country.

On November 19th, 1863 a memorial to those killed at Gettysburg was held at the battlefield. President Lincoln gave a short speech that later became known as the Gettysburg Address.

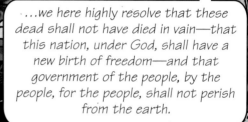

...we here highly resolve that these dead shall not have died in vain—that this nation, under God, shall have a new birth of freedom—and that government of the people, by the people, for the people, shall not perish from the earth.

FAST FACT Lincoln's Gettysburg address was just ten sentences long and had only 272 words.

The American Civil War is characterised by its many battles and immense number of casualties. It also marks a turning point in US history concerning slavery. This timeline and facts section will try to shed light on some of the battles preceeding Gettysburg and pinpoint important dates during this period of time, as well as filling some factual gaps.

July 4 1783: *American rebels secure US independence from Britain*

November 6 1860: *Abraham Lincoln is elected president*

December 20 1860: *South Carolina leaves the Union*

January 1861: *Further states in the south leave the Union: Florida, Alabama, Georgia, Louisiana, Texas, Arkansas and Tennessee*

February 18 1861: *Jefferson Davis becomes president of the Confederacy*

April 12 1861: *Attack on Fort Sumter begins; Lincoln orders all Southern ports to be blockaded*

July 21 1861: *First Battle of Bull Run Northern troops fail to capture the Southern capital of Richmond, Virginia*

April 25 1862: *Union captures New Orleans, which allows them to move up the Mississippi River*

August 29-30 1862: *Second Battle of Bull Run*

A large Northern force is trapped by combined Confederate forces

September 22 1862: *Lincoln announces emancipation of slaves, freeing all slaves of the Confederacy and thus reducing the available manpower in the South*

December 13 1862: *Battle of Fredericksburg*

Unsuccessful attempt by the Northern army to capture the town of Fredericksburg, Virginia, from a heavily outnumbered Southern army

May 1-4 1863: *Battle of Chancellorsville The Union Army of the Potomac is defeated by the Confederate Army of Northern Virginia at the Battle of Chancellorsville west of Fredericksburg, Virginia*

July 1-3 1863: *Battle of Gettysburg*

Battle which marks the turning point of the American Civil War. Consists of a series of engagements taking place between Union and Confederate troops at Gettysburg, Pennsylvania. There are heavy losses on both sides - Union: 23,000; Confederacy: 25,000

November 19 1863: *Lincoln's Gettysburg Address*

November 8 1864: *Lincoln is reelected as president*

April 9 1865: *General Lee surrenders at Appomattox Court House*

April 14 1865: *Lincoln shot. He dies the next day and is succeeded by Andrew Johnson*

May 10 1865: *Jefferson Davis captured by Confederate troops*

May 10 1865: *President Johnson declares the Civil War at an end*

1 *There were about 4 million slaves in the south in 1860. The number of slaves was growing even though it was illegal to import new slaves.*

2 *Many states had their own small armies which were called "militias". It was sometimes difficult to get them to work together.*

3 *Lincoln did not grow a beard until he ran for president in 1860.*

4 *The nickname for a confederate soldier was "Johnny Reb". Union soldiers were called "Billy Yank".*

5 *At the start of the war, a Union private earned $13 a month. A Confederate soldier earned $11 a month.*

6 *Soldiers on both sides of the war called going into combat "seeing the elephant". "Elephant" meant any kind of fighting, large or small.*

7 *In 1861 the U.S. Congress started collecting income tax to help pay for the war. It ended in 1872.*

8 *American sailors who were seasick were said "to pay tribute to Neptune".*

9 *The Union named its armies after rivers in areas where they fought, like the Army of the Potomac. Confederate armies were named after states such as the Army of Northern Virginia.*

10 *The American poet Ralph Waldo Emerson wrote a poem called "Boston Hymn" to celebrate the emancipation of slaves.*

11 *Even though slaves could become soldiers their officers were nearly always white.*

12 *The cannon at Gettysburg were so loud that they could be heard over 150 miles away.*

13 *It is estimated that over 400 women disguised themselves as men to fight in the war.*

14 *The last battle of the Civil War was fought on May 13 1865 at Palmito Ranch, Texas. The Confederates won.*

15 *Sickness accounted for a full one-third of all casualties in the Civil War. In some cases over 40% of the soldiers of a regiment were taken ill before their first engagement.*

16 *Over 10,000 soldiers serving in the Union Army were under the age of 18.*

17 *The commander of the Confederate forces, General Lee, travelled with a pet hen that laid one egg under his cot every morning.*

18 *Black soldiers were paid $10 per month while serving in the Union army. This was $3 less than white soldiers.*

19 *Approximately 130,000 freed slaves became Union soldiers during the war.*

20 *During the time of the Civil War, surgeons never washed their hands or instruments after an operation, because all blood was assumed to be the same.*

21 *President Abraham Lincoln was the first president of the United States to be assassinated.*

Abolition: *The act of stopping slavery.*

Ammunition: *Objects fired from weapons such as bullets, cannon balls and rockets.*

Arsenal: *A place to make and store weapons and ammunition.*

Artillery: *The heavy, mounted missiles of an army, in particular the longer-range weapons that cannot be carried by soldiers.*

Bayonet: *A long knife attached to the end of a rifle. It was used to defeat enemies in close combat.*

Campaign: *A series of military operations during a war.*

Cavalry: *Troops that fight on horseback.*

Combat: *Fighting, especially between armed forces*

Commemorate: *To honour an event or person with a ceremony.*

Confederacy: *An alliance of the southern states of America from 1860 to 1863.*

Constitution: *A number of fundamental principles and ideas according to which a state or organization is governed.*

Defensive: *Getting prepared for an attack - usually by building walls or digging tranches.*

Federal: *During the Civil War, a supporter of the government.*

Flag officer: *An historic rank within the navy; it describes a senoir officer above the rank of captain. This corresponds to the term General Officer used by land forces to describe all grades of Generals.*

Fleet: *A group of warships acting together as a unit and capable of strategic positioning.*

Fort: *An extremely stable building or strategic position used in warfare as a shelter or arms depository.*

General: *A commander of an army, or an army officer ranking above lieutenant general.*

Iron clad ship: *A warship that is either partly or entirely clad in iron.*

Major-general: *A rank of officer in the army, above brigadier or brigadier general and below lieutenant general.*

Manufacturing: *The process of making (something), especially on a large scale using machinery.*

Militia: *An army of volunteers who are not professional soldiers.*

Mississippi River: *River that rises in Minnesota and then flows south, following the boundaries between the states of Minnesota, Iowa, Missouri, Arkansas, and Louisiana on the west, and Wisconsin, Illinois, Kentucky, Tennessee, and Mississippi on the east. The Mississippi River, 3,779 km (2,348* mi) long, is the second longest river, after the Missouri, in the United States. The river, whose name means "father of waters" in the Algonquian language, has long been an important transportation artery of North America.

New Orleans: *New Orleans was founded by the French in 1718 and has played an important role in the history of the United States. The city was named in honor of Philip II, Duke of Orléans, who was regent and ruler of France when the city was founded. It is a major U.S. port city and historically the largest city in the U.S. state of Louisiana. It is located in southeastern Louisiana along the Mississippi River, just south of Lake Pontchartrain.*

Plantation: *A large estate on which crops such as coffee, sugar, cotton and tobacco are grown. Plantations in the Confederate regions owned slaves to grow these crops.*

President: *The head of a government.*

Proclamation: *An official announcement.*

Rifle: *A gun, especially one fired from shoulder level, having a long spirally grooved barrel to make a bullet spin and thereby increase accuracy over a long distance.*

Searing: *Burning or scorching with a sudden intense heat.*

Secede: *To break away or leave something. During the Civil War the southern states seceded from the United States.*

Siege: *A town or fortress surrounded by an army that wants to capture it.*

Slavery: *One person is the property of another.*

Treaty: *A formal agreement between two countries.*

Troop: *A unit of soldiers or armed forces.*

Union: *During the Civil War, states that did not secede from the United States.*

Virginia: *The Commonwealth of Virginia is one of the original thirteen states of the United States that revolted against British rule in the American Revolution, and is part of the South. It is one of four states that use the name commonwealth. Virginia was the first part of the Americas to be colonized permanently by England. Kentucky and West Virginia were part of Virginia at the time of the founding of the United States, but the former was admitted to the Union as a separate state in 1792, while the latter broke away from Virginia during the American Civil War.*

INDEX

A

America
  independence 4–5
  north–south divide 8–12
  slavery 6–7
army names 45
artillery 29, 32–33, 35, 37, 46

B

Battle of the Bull Run 13
Battle of Chancellorville 17
Battle of Gettysburg
  Day One 20–25
  Day Two 26–31
  Day Three 32–43
Battle of Hampton Roads 15
bayonets 23, 31, 37, 46
Big Round Top 27–29
black soldiers 45

C

cannons 28–29, 33, 45
casualties 17, 21, 35, 37, 42, 45
Cemetery Ridge 24, 32–37
Clark, William 5
Confederacy 2, 12, 46
Constitution 4, 46
cotton 7, 8, 42
crops 11, 42

D

Davis, Jefferson 2, 12, 18
Devil's Den 27

E

earnings 45
emancipation 2, 45

Europe 18

F

factories 9
Farragut, Flag Officer 14–15
First Battle of the Bull Run 13
Flag Officer 14–15, 46
food 19
Fort Sumter 12
forts 14, 46

G

Gettysburg Address 43
government 4, 10–11
Grant, Ulysses 2, 39–41

H

Hancock, Winfield 24–25
hand-to-hand fighting 13, 23, 27
Hooker, Joseph 16–17, 19

I

income tax 45
iron-clad ships 15, 46

J

Jackson, Thomas J. (Stonewall) 2, 17

K

Kemper, General 36

L

Lee, Robert E. 2, 16–18, 20, 32–35, 39–40, 45
Lewis, Meriwether 5
Lincoln, Abraham 2, 12, 19, 45
Little Round Top 27, 29–31
Louisiana Purchase 4–5

M

McPherson's Ridge 22–25
manufacturing 9, 46
Meade, George C. 2, 19–20
militias 45, 46
Mississippi River 5, 8, 14, 46–47

N

New Orleans 14–15, 47
north–south divide 8–12

P

Palmito Ranch 45
Pickett, General 33–35
Pickett's Charge 2, 34–35

R

railways 9
Reynolds, John 21
rifles 37, 47

S

Seminary Ridge 25
ships 15
sickness 45
slaves and slavery 2, 6–7, 42, 45, 47
surgeons 45
surrender 39

U

Union 2, 47

V

Virginia 16–17, 47

W

Washington, George 4
women 45